THE CHURCH

TOPIC 1 – The Universal Church

Key Points

- The word "church" is used in scripture to designate the totality of believers from the Day of Pentecost in AD33 to the Return of Christ at the Rapture.

- The word is also used for a group of Christians who meet in a locality to bear testimony to Christ by observing the Lord's Supper, preaching the gospel, baptising converts and engaging in prayer.

- Neither Old Testament saints nor those saved after the Rapture belong to the Church.

- A better translation of the word church is "assembly"..

In this study we will concentrate on what the Bible calls "the Church which is His body" (Eph. 1:22-23) sometimes described as the Universal Church or the Dispensational Church.

To most people the church is a building with a spire and possibly a graveyard. Or it may mean a religious organisation with headquarters and a leader. But the bible does not support either of these meanings. In the NT the word church is used as a collective expression covering all Christians from the Day of Pentecost in Acts 2 to the return of Christ or a gathering of Christians in a locality. These two usages are seen in the following passages -

> [18] And I say also unto thee, That thou art Peter, and upon this rock I will build my church; and the gates of hell shall not prevail against it.
>
> **Matthew 16:18**

> [15] Moreover if thy brother shall trespass against thee, go and tell him his fault ... if he will not hear *thee, then* take with thee one or two more.....
> [17] And if he shall neglect to hear them, tell *it* unto the church: but if he neglect to hear the church, let him be unto thee as an heathen man and a publican.
>
> **Matthew 18:15**

The first passage refers the whole body of believers. We will call it the Church, with a capital "C". The second refers to an assembly of Christians who gather in a particular area. Unlike the Church which is a spiritual body with no physical location and which spans a vast period of time, the local church has a defined membership, and as Matthew 18 shows, can be marred by disunity, and may have to discipline it members. The church in Matthew 18 may be depleted and discouraged whereas the Church of Matthew 16 cannot be defeated nor can it be overcome.

The Church - its Constituents

In most translations of the Bible the word "church" is used to translate the Greek word *ekklesia*. This is a little strange because *ekklesia* means "assembly" or "gathering". Why then is the word "church" used? It seems that the early Christians in the English-speaking world referred to the place Christians met as a *kuriakos*, a Greek word meaning "belonging to God". This word was anglicised and became "church". The Scottish word "kirk" is derived from *kuriakos*. The word "church" became so firmly established in the English language that the translators of the first English bibles did not attempt to translate church literally as "assembly" or "gathering". This is a pity because the word "assembly" reveals the true meaning of scripture. The church is a "people belonging to God". *Ekklesia* is a composite of two Greek words *ek* – "out of" and *klesis* – a calling; the *ekklesia* is therefore a calling out and by implication a gathering together.

Local churches gather on earth. The Church will be gathered together in the air when the Lord Jesus returns. A local church gathers as an assembly and then separates until the next meeting. When Christ comes to the air the Church will "gather together unto Him" (2 Thess. 2:1) and never part again.

The Church – its Commencement

Although the Lord Jesus anticipated the formation of the Church in His ministry there is no description of a gathering of believers in church capacity prior to the day of Pentecost in Acts ch 2. The supernatural events described in Acts 2 marked the inception of the Church. Although the Spirit fell on the believers who constituted the first local church that baptism was symbolic of the formation of the Universal Church. Although it is correct to say that the word "baptism" is not used in Acts 2 to describe what occurred, Peter later (Acts 11:15-16) describes the events of Acts 2 as "baptism with the Spirit". While some think that every time a believer is saved he/she is baptised in the Spirit, the prophecies of this baptism by John the Baptist seem to assume one not many baptisms. Moreover 1 Cor. 12:13 indicates that the baptism in the Spirit is something which unites every type of believer in one body. If baptism is a personal experience it is difficult to see why it should signify the unity of believers from every background and race. It should also be noted that in Acts 2 the people in the house who saw and heard the Spirit descending were already believers. So it was not a conversion experience for them.

The Church – its Conclusion

The bible teaches that one day the Lord will return to the air and snatch away from the earth the living Christians and resurrect the dead Christians of the Church age (1 Thess. 4:16-17). The word "rapture" is not found in the bible. It is the anglicisation of the Latin verb *rapto*. This word was used in Latin versions of the bible to translate the Greek word *harpazō*, the word used in 1 Thess. 4:17 to describe the snatching or carrying away of the Christians from earth. Rapture is therefore a term that describes the snatching away of the Church.

Although God will continue to work on earth after the Rapture, the Book of Revelation, which describes this period from ch 4-19, never mentions the church. John does however refer to Israel and the nations of earth. Thus it seems the Church age ends with the Rapture. Whether the saints who belong to the Church and who are taken to heaven ever set foot on earth again is debatable. Certainly the Head of the Church returns to earth – so if the Church never returns to earth He must leave His bride behind! Although the events of Rev. ch20-22 are notoriously difficult to interpret it seems that the New Jerusalem descends to earth. If the Church inhabits the New Jerusalem then the Church does appear to return (eventually) to the earth in the post-Millennium phase of earth's existence. This period is sometimes called the eternal state.

The Church – its Characteristics

Its members are composed of all Christians wherever they are found. Even those who are put out of the local church for a serious sin remain part of the universal Church. Apart from salvation there is no other condition of membership. Unbaptised believers belong to it. Carnal Christians belong to it. It embraces the young and the old. It is a complete entity that knows no denominational division. Christians from all backgrounds and whatever allegiance, all belong to this Church.

Here are some features that distinguish it from a local church.

1. It has never physically met together. On the Day of Pentecost when the church "began" there were believers who were not in Jerusalem or even in the Upper Room (Acts 1:13; 2:1). When the Spirit descended all believers then alive made the transition from Old Covenant ground into membership of the new body called the Church.

2. It has no human leadership. Its only leader is Christ, who is the "head of the Church".

3. Its numbers never decrease nor can it go out of existence, unlike local churches.

The Church will gradually increase in its numerical composition until it reaches full maturity and is taken to heaven (Eph. 2:21; 1 Pet. 2:5). In Paul's writings the Church is sometimes viewed as a complete entity that needs no growth e.g. Eph. 1:22-23.

Here are some characteristics that distinguish it from Israel –

1. The Church has no headquarters, or physical location. Israel had a temple, a city and a land that was the hub for its religious and political activity.

2. The Church has no ethnic identity. It is drawn from every race under the sun. Israel by contrast was an ethnic group.

3. The Church was brought into relationship with God through the Gospel whereas Israel was brought into existence by natural birth and bound to God at Sinai by the Old Covenant.

The Church is different from Israel and has not replaced it in any way (see 1 Cor. 10:32; Eph. 2:12; Rom. 11:12).

The Church - its Comparisons

The Church is described in a number of ways. It is described as a Building (Eph. 2:20-22; 1 Pet. 2:5), a Body (Eph. 1:22-23; 1 Cor. 12:13; Col. 1:18), a Bride (Eph. 5:31-32; Rev. 21:9), a Flock (John 10:16), a City (Rev. 21:2) and a Man (Eph. 2:15).

These images are meant to convey the unity, purity and attractiveness of the Church to the Lord Jesus.

 KEY SCRIPTURES

> [18] And hath put all *things* under his feet, and gave him to be the head over all *things* to the church, [23] Which is his body, the fulness of him that filleth all in all.
>
> **Ephesians 1:22-23**

> [25] Husbands, love your wives, even as Christ also loved the church, and gave himself for it; [26] That he might sanctify and cleanse it

with the washing of water by the word, [27] That he might present it to himself a glorious church, not having spot, or wrinkle, or any such thing; but that it should be holy and without blemish.

Ephesians 5:25

[18] And he is the head of the body, the church: who is the beginning, the firstborn from the dead; that in all *things* he might have the preeminence.

Colossians 1:18

[4] For he is our peace, who hath made both one, and hath broken down the middle wall of partition *between us*....... for to make in himself of twain one new man, *so* making peace;...... [19] Now therefore ye are no more strangers and foreigners, but fellowcitizens with the saints, and of the household of God; [20] And are built upon the foundation of the apostles and prophets, Jesus Christ himself being the chief corner *stone*; [21] In whom all the building fitly framed together groweth unto an holy temple in the Lord: [22] In whom ye also are builded together for an habitation of God through the Spirit.

Ephesians 2:4,19-21

[5] Ye also, as lively stones, are built up a spiritual house, an holy priesthood, to offer up spiritual sacrifices, acceptable to God by Jesus Christ..... [9] But ye *are* a chosen generation, a royal priesthood, an holy nation, a peculiar people; that ye should shew forth the praises of him who hath called you out of darkness into his marvellous light: [10] Which in time past *were* not a people, but *are* now the people of God: which had not obtained mercy, but now have obtained mercy.

1 Peter 2:5, 9-10

[1] And when the day of Pentecost was fully come, they were all with one accord in one place. [2] And suddenly there came a sound from heaven as of a rushing mighty wind, and it filled all the house where

KEY SCRIPTURES

they were sitting. ³ And there appeared unto them cloven tongues like as of fire, and it sat upon each of them. ⁴ And they were all filled with the Holy Ghost, and began to speak with other tongues, as the Spirit gave them utterance.

³⁸ Then Peter said unto them, Repent, and be baptized every one of you in the name of Jesus Christ for the remission of sins, and ye shall receive the gift of the Holy Ghost.... ⁴¹ Then they that gladly received his word were baptized: and the same day there were added *unto them* about three thousand souls..... ⁴² And they continued stedfastly in the apostles' doctrine and fellowship, and in breaking of bread, and in prayers..... And the Lord added to the church daily such as should be saved.

Acts 2:1-4, 38, 40-42 and 47

¹³ For by one Spirit are we all baptized into one body, whether *we be* Jews or Gentiles, whether *we be* bond or free; and have been all made to drink into one Spirit.

1 Corinthians 12:13

¹³ But we do not want you to be uninformed, brothers, about those who are asleep, that you may not grieve as others do who have no hope. ¹⁴ For since we believe that Jesus died and rose again, even so, through Jesus, God will bring with him those who have fallen asleep. ¹⁵ For this we declare to you by a word from the Lord, that we who are alive, who are left until the coming of the Lord, will not precede those who have fallen asleep. ¹⁶ For the Lord himself will descend from heaven with a cry of command, with the voice of an archangel, and with the sound of the trumpet of God. And the dead in Christ will rise first. ¹⁷ Then we who are alive, who are left, will be caught up together with them in the clouds to meet the Lord in the air, and so we will always be with the Lord. ¹⁸ Therefore encourage one another with these words.

1 Thessalonians 4:13-18 (E.S.V.)

KEY QUOTES

The book of Acts speaks frequently of the 'church' (nineteen times) and 'Israel' (twenty times). However, 'church' refers to those believing at Pentecost and beyond; while 'Israel' refers to the nation—historically and ethnically. The terms are never used synonymously or interchangeably. The church is never called 'spiritual Israel' or 'new Israel' in the New Testament; furthermore Israel is never called 'the church' in the Old Testament. There are really only three texts that might even remotely be considered to equate Israel with the church.

1. Romans 9:6 - distinguishes between physical birth and the new birth.
2. Romans 11:26, which promises that all elect Jews will be saved.
3. Galatians 6:16, which refers to the believing Jews in the Galatian congregations.

'Church' is mentioned at least eighteen times in Revelation chapters 1–3. It is not later confused with 'Israel' in Revelation chapters 6–19. Between Revelation 3:22 and Revelation 22:16, there is no mention of the church. Only Futuristic Pre-millennialism accounts for this clear Biblical distinction.[1]

Richard Mayhue

For a Christian to fail to participate in the life of a local church is inexcusable. In fact, those who choose to isolate themselves are disobedient to the direct command of Scripture. Hebrews 10:24-25 charges believers to "consider how to stimulate one another to love and good deeds, not forsaking our own assembling together, as is the habit of some, but encouraging one another; and all the more, as you see the day drawing near." The Bible does not envision the Christian life as one lived apart from other believers. All members of the universal church, the body of Christ, are to be actively and intimately involved in local assemblies.[2]

John MacArthur

[1] Mayhue, R. *1 & 2 Thessalonians: Triumphs and Trials of a Consecrated Church pp. 218–219.*
[2] John MacArthur, MacArthur New Testament Commentary – Acts 1-12 p. 84.

KEY QUESTIONS

1. Does the expression the "church which is His body" refer to a local assembly or all believers from Pentecost to the Rapture?

2. When does a Christian enter the Universal Church?

3. When is the Church taken to heaven?

4. What are the differences between the Church and Israel?

TOPIC 2 - THE LOCAL CHURCH

 Key Points
- The first assembly was formed in Jerusalem on the Day of Pentecost.
- The first assembly's unity was based on adherence to key doctrinal truths and submission to the authority of the apostles.
- Although the local assembly has many functions its primary function is to promote the cause of Christ.
- The fact that a group is called a "church" is no guarantee that they practise the truths that were characteristic of the early churches.

The Church - The Formation of the church

The first local church was constituted in Jerusalem on the Day of Pentecost in AD 33 about ten days after the Lord's return to heaven.[3] We know this because Acts 2:41 and 47 tells us that the people who were saved that day were added to the "church" in Jerusalem. The assembly was initially composed of twelve apostles[4], the women who had supported the Lord during His earthly ministry, His brothers (Acts 1:13-14) and other unknown believers, making in total 120 people (Acts 1:15). Over ten years later the apostles and the Lord's brethren were still in the assembly in Jerusalem and had not returned to Galilee or Nazareth etc. (Acts 15:4, 13). Although assemblies were formed in these places (Acts 9:31) they recognised that God had joined them to the Jerusalem assembly and they did not it seems return to Galilee to join assemblies formed there. This may well

---

[3] About 50 days after 4 April AD33, the day the Lord was crucified.
[4] Matthias having just been appointed to take Judas's place (Acts 1:26).

have been because they appreciated that the assembly is a cohesive body (1 Cor. 12:12; 1 Pet. 2:5) and not a loose association from which one may come and go.

The first assembly meeting was memorable. The Lord had told the disciples to wait in Jerusalem for the fulfilment of His promise that He would baptise them with the Spirit (Acts 1:4-5). As they waited a great wind filled the house and flames of fire appeared above the believers' heads (Acts 2:1-3). This was the fulfilment of John the Baptist's words -

> I indeed have baptized you with water: but he shall baptize you with the Holy Ghost.
>
> **Mk 1:8**

The Church - The Form of the church

Luke gives us a glimpse of the defining features of the early church in Acts 2. They provide a useful template for assemblies today.

> 41 Then they that gladly received his word were baptised: and the same day there were added *unto them* about three thousand souls. 42 And they continued stedfastly in the apostles' doctrine and fellowship, and in breaking of bread, and in prayers.
>
> **Acts 2:41-42**

In total seven features are mentioned by Luke. These are (1) that the church is composed of people who have been saved and (2) baptised and who (3) are added to the assembly. They (4) adhere to the apostles' doctrine (5) are in fellowship with one another, (6) break bread in remembrance of the Lord Jesus and (7) practise collective prayer. The truths covered by "the apostles' doctrine" are not defined, no doubt because they were too numerous to list. For the church today the apostles' doctrine is found in scripture which is a record of the doctrine taught by Paul, Peter and John, the leading apostles.

The "apostles' doctrine" includes the following core truths -

- The Lord Jesus is a member of a trinity of Father, Son and Holy Spirit, became flesh when Mary his mother conceived and was born while Mary was a virgin;

- The Lord Jesus is fully God and fully man; lived a sinless life, died for the sins of the world, rose, ascended and is coming again;

- Salvation is received by faith in Christ;

- After salvation believers should be baptised by immersion;

- The church is composed of those who are saved and baptised and who are not guilty of moral sin or believe serious doctrinal error; and

- The church should be characterised by the exercise of the gifts of the Spirit and scriptural order including properly constituted church leadership and the recognition of headship.

The Church - The Fundamentals of the church

When is a church not a church? The best way to answer this is with an illustration. How do we recognise an elephant? Although there are many animals the elephant has a distinctive combination of characteristics - a trunk, two large ears, a large body, four legs and tail. Even although a giraffe also has a large body, four legs and a tail its ears are not as large as an elephant and it has no trunk. Thus while it may share some features of an elephant it is not an elephant. That is not to say that all elephants are identical. A baby elephant is still an elephant even though it is smaller than an adult elephant. An African elephant differs from an Asian elephant but both are elephants.

In recognising an assembly we look for key characteristics. If these are lacking it is not appropriate to describe the group or organisation as a church. The test is not whether the group or organisation calls itself a church. Nor is the test whether or not the people in the group are saved or preach the gospel. The bible makes it abundantly clear that a church is far more than a group of Christians who are saved (see above).

Although a church constituted according to the scriptures will have uniform features, they are by no manner of means clones. Some meet in well appointed halls, others under trees. Some gather to break bread as the sun rises, others meet in the evening after work. They sing from a myriad of different hymnbooks. They read from a variety of translations in a variety of languages. A doctrinal code covering the minutiae of assembly life is never envisaged by scripture. We must be careful therefore not to impose rules that are of our own devising and allow assemblies freedom to adapt to their circumstances subject to the unifying principles of scripture.

Many denominations teach that salvation is imparted by infant baptism or through eating the wafer or drinking the cup at services described variously as the Mass, Communion or the Eucharist. They preach a gospel of works and not faith. In the Reformed Churches conversion is not a prerequisite of church membership and they practise sprinkling rather than baptism by immersion. In other denominations the deviation from the apostles' doctrine is not so much in connection with the gospel as basic church truth. Women do not cover their heads and may participate in public prayer or preaching, the congregation speak in "tongues" – all in contravention of clear scripture. While the degree of deviation from the truth may vary, the word "church" in its New Testament sense cannot be applied to bodies that have so few of the hallmarks of the apostolic church.

Some of the activities performed by the church can be performed by both individuals and the assembly. Thus we engage in private prayer at home as well as public prayer at assembly gatherings. Missionaries preach the gospel and instruct converts on their own before an assembly is planted. But preaching is also done within the confines of the assembly. The breaking of bread is different. After the Church was formed the Lord's Supper was always observed by assemblies of believers – the apostle never broke bread (in the ecclesiastical sense) on his own or with his companions.

It is appropriate to say a word or two about "para-church" organisations. These abound in Christendom. Where they usurp the function of the church they can seriously debilitate testimony. Time and money that could strengthen local assemblies are diverted into organisations that provide an alternative to the church. That is not to say that all such organisations are detrimental to testimony. Where they provide support for the church, they perform useful service. Some trusts (e.g. the Lord's Work Trust – a trust organised to forward gifts to evangelists and missionaries) and societies (e.g. Missionary Aviation Fellowship - a body created to provide air transport for missionaries). do not detract from the role designated in scripture for assemblies.

Scripture does not say what the minimum or maximum size of an assembly should be. The expression "where two or three are gathered together in My Name" (Matt. 18:19) ought not to be regarded as fixing the minimum size of an assembly at either two or three[5]. The assembly at Jerusalem appears to have had three thousand in fellowship in Acts 2 and to have grown still further thereafter. That may have been however a temporary state of affairs since at that time there was no other local assembly and its numbers were swollen by people who were visiting Jerusalem.

The Church – The Focus of the church

Although the sections above have focused on doctrines that (regrettably) divide Christians, it is nevertheless true that the primary purpose of the church is to honour God and serve Christ. It does this by spreading the gospel, breaking bread in memory of Christ, conducting itself in a way that reflects the love of Christ for the Church and the world. It also seeks to commit itself wholeheartedly to the truth.

KEY SCRIPTURES

[11] I indeed baptize you with water unto repentance: but he that cometh after me is mightier than I, whose shoes I am not worthy to bear: he shall baptize you with the Holy Ghost, and *with* fire.

Matt. 3:11

[16] John answered, saying unto *them* all, I indeed baptize you with water; but one mightier than I cometh, the latchet of whose shoes I am not worthy to unloose: he shall baptize you with the Holy Ghost and with fire.

Lk 3:16

[5] The context of the passage indicates that "two or three" signifies a small group of believers who have met to deal with a problem that has arisen between two brethren (v15). There is no reason however why promise of the presence of Christ should not be true of other gatherings of believers. Thus provided an assembly meets "in His name" i.e. in acknowledgement of His authority over them in matters of doctrine and practice, the Lord is spiritually present.

KEY SCRIPTURES

¹ And when the day of Pentecost was fully come, they were all with one accord in one place. ² And suddenly there came a sound from heaven as of a rushing mighty wind, and it filled all the house where they were sitting. ³ And there appeared unto them cloven tongues like as of fire, and it sat upon each of them. ⁴ And they were all filled with the Holy Ghost, and began to speak with other tongues, as the Spirit gave them utterance.

Acts 2:1-4

¹³ For by one Spirit are we all baptized into one body, whether *we be* Jews or Gentiles, whether *we be* bond or free; and have been all made to drink into one Spirit.

1 Cor. 12:13

For in one Spirit were we all baptized into one body, whether Jews or Greeks, whether bond or free; and were all made to drink of one Spirit.

1 Cor. 12:13 (RV)

....the house of God... is the church of the living God, the pillar and ground of the truth.

1 Tim. 3:15

KEY QUOTES

After the first century, the churches... began to slide into conformity with the world.... By the time of the Reformation the gospel of grace was buried under ritualism .... Salvation was viewed as a life-long process of keeping the rules of the church and at death one went to purgatory to atone for... sins....The Reformation rediscovered the gospel of God's grace and proclaimed it faithfully. Unfortunately, many of those reformers did not make a clean break with all Romish practices. They carried over into their churches the teaching of infant baptism, the clergy-laity concept and the desire to have a state church.

Throughout church history there have been repeated movements to return to the simplicity of the early church... (whose) example was viewed not as an historical oddity but as the norm for churches in every age.

Donald Norbie[6]

'The church which is his body', Eph.1. 22, 23, is inclusive of every true believer in Christ of the whole dispensation since the day of Pentecost, Acts 2, until the coming to the air of the Lord Jesus and the translation to heaven of all the saved. By the baptism in the spirit, 1 Cor. 12. 12, 13, every believer has been brought into a unity of life eternal in the risen, ascended Lord, enthroned at the right Hand of God. That church is one. Therefore we never read of 'the churches which are His bodies'. The term 'church of God', is used in a plural form, the Holy Spirit thus designating the local companies of the saints.

Willie Trew[7]

[6] "Blurring the Distinctives" Precious Seed 2002 Issue 2.
[7] "The Church of God" Precious Seed 1945.

KEY QUESTIONS

1. What does gathering "in the name" of the Lord Jesus mean? What scripture is this phrase based on?

2. What are the main points of the "apostles' doctrine"?

3. Where was the first local assembly formed?

4. Have all Christians the right to be a member of the local assembly? If not why not?

TOPIC 3 –
The Church and its Fellowship

Key Points
- The assembly is a place where the believers have fellowship with each other.
- Fellowship involves sharing a common salvation in Christ, believing the same essential truths, and being willing to use personal possessions for the benefit of fellow believers.
- Salvation does not bring a believer into assembly fellowship.

Assembly fellowship – Its content

As we noticed in the last study "fellowship" characterised the church in Jerusalem (Acts 2:42). The word means "sharing in common". For these Christians fellowship meant sharing their talents, possessions and time with other Christians in the assembly. This is the N.T. ideal. If a person wants to "enter fellowship" or be "in fellowship" it means being fully involved in the life of the assembly. It is not a ticket to the breaking of bread or entry on a roll of members. Someone who rarely attends the gatherings or contributes nothing to the assembly, is not truly in fellowship. Of course sometimes ill health or age and other factors can limit the degree of fellowship. We should also be slow to measure fellowship by purely material or visible indicators. Someone who faithfully prays for the assembly is in fellowship even though he or she may be unable to attend the gatherings.

Fellowship is closely connected to "membership". This refers to the idea that we are all members of one body (1 Cor. 12:12-27). Fellowship and membership stress the interdependence that ought to exist between those who are part of the local assembly.

Assembly fellowship – Its character

Fellowship is the "glue" that sticks an assembly together. It has a number of ingredients -

- Sharing salvation. We have each experienced new birth and because of God's work in our lives have a host of common characteristics that are absent in our worldly friends.

- Sharing beliefs. Common convictions enable us to "walk together" in harmony (Amos 3:3). The church at Jerusalem was held together by its commitment to the "apostles' doctrine" not just by friendship or habit.

- Sharing a status. We have been placed into the body as members. The local assembly has been brought together by divine design (1 Cor. 12:12-27).

- Sharing possessions. The church in Jerusalem pooled their resources and gave away personal possessions (Acts 2:44). Although other churches mentioned in the Acts of the Apostles and the churches described in the epistles do not seem to have shared resources to the same extent as the church at Jerusalem, there is no doubt that the assemblies of the N.T. era shared their food, homes and possessions with their fellow believers as a practical expression of their fellowship with one another.

There is of course fellowship with believers everywhere (1 Cor. 1:9) since our common life in Christ unites us. This fellowship however is not co-extensive with assembly fellowship. Assembly fellowship requires agreement on key issues of doctrine and practice. If that agreement is lacking united testimony is impossible.

Assembly fellowship – Its collapse

Sometimes moral wrongdoing (1 Cor. 5:1-5) or serious misbehaviour (2 Thess. 3:11-15) or doctrinal error (2 Tim. 2:16-17, 20-21) requires fellowship to be withdrawn or refused. Personal circumstances also can prevent a believer from being in fellowship. Elderly saints may be forced to live with children who are not believers and who do not or cannot take them to an assembly. It is also possible to have no assembly to go to. The Ethiopian eunuch was converted en route to Ethiopia. There is no reason to think that once he got home he had an assembly to go to. We simply do not know whether in his lifetime an assembly was planted in Ethiopia – what we know of that region might dispose us to think he never had the privilege of assembly fellowship.

Assembly fellowship – Its criteria

It is clear that church gatherings are public not private affairs. Paul notes in 1st Corinthians that visitors may attend an assembly gathering. Thus he refers to the attendance of the "unlearned" and the "unbeliever" at the gatherings in 1 Cor. 14:23. It is instructive that unlearned believers were not regarded as part of the church. He contrasts the "whole church" with these outsiders; cf. 1 Cor. 5:12-13. In other words the local assembly is not a loose association of all Christians who happen to be in attendance at a gathering but a body with a defined membership. Although it is apparent from Paul's first epistle to the Corinthians that they had serious deficiencies in their knowledge of (e.g. about marriage, association with pagan temples, the Lord's Supper and the miraculous gifts of the Spirit) they were still in fellowship with one another. The unlearned were probably saved but lacked understanding of the key points of the apostles' doctrine. This needed to be corrected before they could enter fellowship or it may be that the assembly in Corinth needed to speak to them to establish whether they wished to join the assembly and were suitable candidates for membership. Either way fellowship and membership of the assembly in Corinth was not an automatic right for visitors even though they were Christians.

Christians move between churches for a variety of reasons. In order to provide assurance that there is the necessary fellowship in doctrine and practise, churches commend to other churches (Rom. 16:1, 2) where the person is unknown. Letters of commendation are a useful but not necessarily infallible means of assuring assemblies that a visitor is eligible for fellowship. They should be used where the visitor is unknown or not well known in the receiving assembly. It is possible to commend by means other than a letter. The vital thing is to assure the assembly that the visitor is eligible for fellowship.

Assembly fellowship – Its compass

Fellowship between believers is paralleled by fellowship between assemblies. Scripture shows that the assemblies in Macedonia sought to support the assembly in Jerusalem materially. Paul describes this as "fellowship" (2 Cor. 8:7). As part of the obligation to share with Christians, those who are gifted to teach and preach should be willing to use their gift elsewhere if other assemblies indicate a desire to have their help. There are numerous examples in scripture of apostles moving from church to church seeking to encourage and instruct the believers. This task remains just as important today. In this fellowship there should be a spiritual desire on the part of the assembly to obtain help and a parallel desire on the part of the visiting speaker to give help.

The bible teaches that we ought to have fellowship with those that give up their secular employment to preach the gospel. When the first wave of non-apostolic evangelists began to move out with the gospel, John counselled Christians to have fellowship with them by opening their homes and providing support (3 John 6-7). This is "fellowship in the gospel" (Phil. 1:5).

 **KEY SCRIPTURES**

> [9] God *is* faithful, by whom ye were called unto the fellowship of his Son Jesus Christ our Lord.
>
> **1 Cor. 1:9**

> [42] And they continued stedfastly in the apostles' doctrine and fellowship, and in breaking of bread, and in prayers.
>
> **Acts 2:42**

> [14] Be ye not unequally yoked together with unbelievers: for what fellowship hath righteousness with unrighteousness? and what communion hath light with darkness?.... [16] And what agreement hath the temple of God with idols? for ye are the temple of the living God; ... [17] Wherefore come out from among them, and be ye separate, saith the Lord, and touch not the unclean *thing*; and I will receive you, [18] And will be a Father unto you, and ye shall be my sons and daughters, saith the Lord Almighty.
>
> **2 Cor. 6:14–18**

> [16] Else when thou shalt bless with the spirit, how shall he that occupieth the room of the unlearned say Amen at thy giving of thanks, seeing he understandeth not what thou sayest?..... [23] If therefore the whole church be come together into one place, and all speak with tongues, and there come in *those that are* unlearned, or unbelievers, will they not say that ye are mad?
>
> **1 Cor. 14:15–23**

KEY SCRIPTURES

[12] For what have I to do to judge them also that are without? do not ye judge them that are within? [13] But them that are without God judgeth. Therefore put away from among yourselves that wicked person.

1 Cor. 5:12–13

KEY QUOTES

Fellowship is a thing of degrees. With some I may have no fellowship. I am told by Scripture, to have no fellowship with unbelievers or with the unfruitful works of darkness.

But I have *something* in common with all believers. ...When I sing the hymns of Toplady or Horalius Bonar, I have fellowship with these men. I cannot avoid it. It is the linking of soul with soul by the influence of divine truth, and by the outgoing of the affections in response to the love of Christ.....So that I may have, and must have, some fellowship with all who in any measure have a love for the Lord and His word.

Again, with some I have *full* fellowship. .... A scripturally-gathered assembly...is composed of true believers only, and these believers, having been baptized in accordance with the Lord's ordinance in Matt. 28, have been gathered unto the name of Christ, acknowledging Him as their true and only centre..... They have no clergyman to preside over them but meet in the recognition of the common priesthood of believers. For ministry they depend on the gifts whom God has raised up and they recognize the prerogative of the Holy Spirit to administer these gifts. They meet every Lord's Day, in accordance with apostolic example, for the purpose of breaking bread, and the worship which accompanies this ordinance is worship in spirit and in truth. It is the centre of the church's activity..... With such an assembly I may have fullest fellowship.[8]

Andrew Stenhouse

[8] "Fellowship", Precious Seed 1955 Issue 5.

 **KEY QUOTES**

Chuck Swindoll suggests that many Christian groups are like a pack of porcupines on a frigid wintry night. The cold drives us closer together in a tight huddle to keep warm. As we begin to snuggle really close, our sharp quills cause us to jab and prick each other—a condition which forces us apart. But before long we start getting cold, so we move back to warm again, only to stab and puncture each other once more.

> *To dwell above with saints we love,*
> *That will be grace and glory.*
> *To live below with saints we know;*
> *That's another story.*

"How can we break ye olde porcupine syndrome?" asks Swindoll. "The answer in one word is involvement. Or, to use the biblical term, it is *fellowship.*"[9]

Chuck Swindoll

---

[9] Nelson's Complete Book of stories, illustrations, and quotes. p. 332.

KEY QUESTIONS

1. What is the probable effect of fundamental differences of opinion on key issues between people who are in an assembly?

2. Are there essential issues about which everyone in assembly fellowship must be agreed? Give some examples.

3. Is absolute unanimity on all issues possible or necessary for members of a local assembly?

4. What is the point of letters of commendation?

TOPIC 4 – The Church and its Order

Key Points

- God is characterised by orderliness in all He does.
- In the N.T. He has set out an order for the assembly.
- Order requires recognition of scriptural authority and submission to God's will.
- Divine order is not designed to limit human freedom but to maximise the effectiveness of service.

The N.T. teaches that the assembly is a place of order. Corinth was a church where the meetings were confused and disorderly. The apostle Paul wrote to advise them that "all things should be done decently and in order" (1 Cor. 14:40). The idea of order is also seen in Paul's depiction of the assembly as a body where each member has its allotted role (1 Cor. 12:20). Order reflects God's character. The universe is orderly. There are laws that govern its behaviour. In the O.T. in particular the Lord promulgated laws designed to make society orderly. The assembly likewise should be a place of order.

The Church – Creatorial order

God assigned males and females different roles in creation. It is not by accident that women bear children and are physically and biologically designed to nurture children (Gen. 2:22; 3:16). By contrast men are assigned the role of leadership in the home (Eph. 5:23, 25 and 28) and are expected to support their wives and families. This natural order is also visible in the assembly. Hence the apostles were males (Matt. 10:12). Elders are males

(1 Tim. 3:1-2). Teachers and preachers are males (1 Tim. 2:12). It is not that women have no role to play in the assembly. The gifts they have however are not public gifts. This is not due to any idea of inferiority. Scripture affirms the equality of man with woman (1 Cor. 11:11-12). In the gospels the women who followed Christ were characterised by a higher level of fidelity and understanding than their male counterparts. They were the first witnesses of His resurrection. It is a grave mistake to assume that God values the gifts given to men more than those given to women.

The Church – Governmental order

The N.T. teaches that assemblies are subject to the supervision of elders. Those who fulfil this role are also described as overseers.[10] Their role is to lead the assembly. The assembly is expected to submit to their rule (Heb. 13:17) and they in turn should be devoted to the wellbeing of the saints (1 Pet. 5:2, 3). Ideally the assembly should also have a second group of believers called deacons or servants. They are expected to have many of the characteristics of overseers. They may be those who are not yet mature enough to be overseers or those who although they lack some of the qualities for overseership are exercised to help the assembly and devoted to the Lord. It is recognised in scripture that there will always be those who lack the qualifications of elders or deacons.

---

[10] In the NT, "bishop" (episkopos) and "elder" (presbyteros) refer to the same office, as shown by the apostle Paul telling Titus to appoint "elders in every city" and then referring to those same individuals as "bishops" (Titus 1:5, 7). While at Miletus, Paul summoned the elders from the church at Ephesus and then addressed them as "overseers" i.e. episkopos (Acts 20:17, 28). In his Letter to Philippi Paul greeted the "bishops and deacons" (Phil 1:1). The fact that there were numerous bishops at Philippi as well as in Ephesus, shows that the idea that a church or churches should be ruled by one bishop is not a scriptural ideal.

The Church - Natural order

In the O.T. and N.T. it is clear that age should be respected (Ex. 20:12; 1 Tim. 5:8). Hence the younger brethren and sisters are expected to defer to their seniors. Even although the world at times is marked by an anarchic spirit where age and experience count for nothing, the assembly is marked by the honour it gives older brethren and sisters. Of course age is no guarantee of wisdom (Job 32:9) nevertheless the general rule is that the young should respect the old.

The Church - Divine Order

The submission of every Christian to God is the most elementary aspect of order (Eph. 1:22; Col. 1:18). There is submission within the Godhead between Father and Son even though both persons are divine and equal in every respect (1 Cor. 11:3). The assembly ought to display the same complimentary yet submissive relationship that exists between the Father and the Son. Practical expression to God's order is found in obedience to scripture.

The Church - Order and its Consequences

This overall requirement of orderliness necessitates a variety of responses. Meetings should as far as possible begin on time. In some cultures the saints arrive at irregular intervals. A lack of reliable transport or means of knowing the time can explain this. But in our culture there is no excuse for poor timekeeping. Although the phrase "when the hour was come (Jesus) sat down with the twelve" (Luke 22:14) may not be directly in point, it does indicate that the Last Supper was conducted in an orderly way.

As far as possible distractions and disruptions from whatever source they come should be avoided. Mobile phones should be switched off. Although there is a trend to use iPads or tablets instead of copies of the bible, users need to be aware that they can distract the user because of the other functions they perform. A more traditional distraction is a baby or young child. Although it is a good thing to bring children to the assembly, if they are too young to behave then it may be advisable to keep them at home or somewhere where they will not cause disruption. The meeting is after all the "House of God" (1 Tim.

3:15). We first encounter this expression in Genesis 28:17. Although Bethel was not the house of God in the same sense as the temple, it was nevertheless a place where God came close to Jacob. Jacob's response reveals the awe that God's presence engendered.

Order in the conduct of the gatherings does not always require prior arrangement. Thus the prayer meeting and the worship of the believers at the Breaking of Bread are organised to the extent that the time and duration of the meetings are fixed but participation is left to the guidance of the Spirit. Where the exercise of gift is involved whether in ministry or the gospel, scripture permits a measure of organisation. Thus those who can teach and preach can be sent to assemblies in order to give them help (1 Cor. 4:17; 1 Thess. 3:2). Help can be sought (Acts 16:9).[11] The New Testament prophet spoke spontaneously as guided by the Spirit and the form of the meetings accommodated this (1 Cor. 14:26). Since it is possible for those that have no or little gift to take part where meetings for teaching and preaching are left open, some form of control must be exercised. This may be achieved by an admonition from the elders that those who are not fitted to teach should not take part or (since warnings are not always heeded) by inviting suitably equipped speakers to take part. It should be recognised that both are forms of control and both have the laudable aim of preventing the unsuited or ungifted from participating. A regrettable amount of energy is spent debating which is the most scriptural means of organising a meeting. Speaking very broadly the open "system" has the advantage of flexibility and spontaneity whereas the booked "system" improves the variety and quality of participation. They should not be regarded as "systems" but options. Sometimes it is desirable to leave a meeting open and sometimes it is wise to invite a speaker to give help. It is worth remembering that a conference or special ministry meeting is just another assembly gathering. While large gatherings may bring different problems, the same scriptural principles apply. The Spirit is not constrained by anything other than the flesh. The flesh can be evident at both open and arranged meetings. In all these things the watchword is "edification" (1 Cor. 14:26).

 KEY SCRIPTURES

> [32] You shall rise before the gray headed and honour the presence of an old man, and fear your God: I *am* the LORD.
>
> **Lev. 19:32**

---

[11] Although the means of sending the invitation then was unusual, the underlying message, "come and help us", is a familiar one. Provided there is mutual exercise and a desire to speak for God, there is no harm in "taking a booking".

KEY SCRIPTURES

³ But I would have you know, that the head of every man is Christ; and the head of the woman *is* the man; and the head of Christ *is* God.

1 Cor. 11:3

²⁶ How is it then, brethren? when ye come together, every one of you hath a psalm, hath a doctrine, hath a tongue, hath a revelation, hath an interpretation. Let all things be done unto edifying. ²⁷ If any man speak in an *unknown* tongue, *let it be* by two, or at the most *by* three, and *that* by course (or "in turn"); and let one interpret. ²⁸ But if there be no interpreter, let him keep silence in the church; and let him speak to himself, and to God. ²⁹ Let the prophets speak two or three, and let the other judge. ³⁰ If *any thing* be revealed to another that sitteth by, let the first hold his peace. ³¹ For ye may all prophesy one by one, that all may learn, and all may be comforted. ³² And the spirits of the prophets are subject to the prophets. ³³ For God is not *the author* of confusion, but of peace, as in all churches of the saints.

³⁴ Let your women keep silence in the churches: for it is not permitted unto them to speak; but they *are commanded* to be under obedience, as also saith the law. ³⁵ And if they will learn any thing, let them ask their husbands at home: for it is a shame for women to speak in the church. ³⁶ What? came the word of God out from you? or came it unto you only? ³⁷ If any man think himself to be a prophet, or spiritual, let him acknowledge that the things that I write unto you are the commandments of the Lord. ³⁸ But if any man be ignorant, let him be ignorant. ³⁹ Wherefore, brethren, covet to prophesy, and forbid not to speak with tongues. ⁴⁰ Let all things be done decently and in order.

1 Cor. 14:26–40

¹⁸ And he is the head of the body, the church: who is the beginning, the firstborn from the dead; that in all *things* he might have the preeminence.

Col 1:18

 **KEY SCRIPTURES**

⁵ For though I be absent in the flesh, yet am I with you in the spirit, joying and beholding your order, and the stedfastness of your faith in Christ.

Col 2:5

¹ Rebuke not an elder, but intreat *him* as a father; *and* the younger men as brethren; ² The elder women as mothers; the younger as sisters, with all purity.

1 Tim. 5:1, 2

¹⁷ Obey them that have the rule over you, and submit yourselves: for they watch for your souls, as they that must give account, that they may do it with joy, and not with grief: for that *is* unprofitable for you.

Heb 13:17

KEY QUOTES

Are there any principles that govern how we should (meet)? There certainly are...
The first is godly order, not confusion. 'Let all things be done decently and in order' is a command from God to the assemblies of His people, as He is 'not the author of confusion but of peace', 1 Cor. 14. 33, 40. ... An 'anything goes' mentality is not of God; after all, 'the spirits of the prophets are subject to the prophets'...
The second principle is that all things should be done to edifying, 1 Cor.14. 26. In other words, public praying, preaching and teaching should be profitable, instructive, and lead to the building-up of believers. ... Others should listen and judge whether the teaching is profitable or not, 1 Cor. 14. 29. No one should be encouraged to preach and teach if they are not gifted to do so. A one-man ministry may be wrong, but so is an any-man ministry... A third and important principle in the order of worship in an assembly meeting is that there should be a clear and distinct difference

¹² Precious Seed 2006.

KEY QUOTES

between the roles of men and women. ....

Ian Rees[12]

The universe is set up in an orderly manner. When was the last time that one of our planets ran into another one? There are billions of stars and planets in the universe, yet they are all in orderly orbits. What are the odds?

- The movement of the planets of our solar system is so precise, scientists can calculate exactly where a planet will be hundreds of years in advance.

- If the earth were farther away from the sun, the climate would be too cold. If it were closer, it would be too hot. If the sun were smaller or larger we would either freeze or roast.

- The moon is on average, 240,000 miles from earth. The gravitational pull from the moon causes the ocean tides that cleanse our shorelines and clean out the shipping channels. If the moon were only 50,000 from earth the gravitational pull from the moon would be so great that the ocean tides would completely submerge the surface of the earth twice per day. A smaller or larger moon would greatly increase of decrease the tides.

- The layer of gases that surround the earth also shows a designer and a sense of order. The atmosphere contains 21% oxygen. If it had 50% or more, any flash of lightening would ignite a forest into fire. If we had less than 10% oxygen, we would not have enough for fire.

- The fact that water expands when it freezes is also by design. Water expands by 9% when it freezes. Most other things contract and get heavier when they freeze. Water freezes and ice floats. This puts a protective layer on the tops of ponds and lakes. If the ice sank to the bottom, all of the life on the pond or lake would freeze and die. The fact that we have water is important also.

Extract from Answers in Genesis

KEY QUESTIONS

1. Which passages of scripture show that elders and overseers are the same people?

2. Are there any circumstances in which a member of an assembly should disobey or defy the elders?

3. What ought the attitude of the young be towards the old?

4. What should our attitude be to the gatherings of the assembly?

TOPIC 5 –
The Church in Christendom

Key Points
- Many major Christian denominations do not accept that faith in Christ is the only means of salvation.
- Many major Christian denominations do not accept that scripture is the sole authority for the church.
- Christendom is marked by ritual and tradition as opposed to fidelity to scripture
- Christendom will one day metamorphose into religious Babylon

Christendom – its development

"Christendom" is an expression that has been used in two ways. It may refer to all churches or religious organisations that claim to follow the Lord Jesus whether in reality or not or it may refer to those nations of the earth over which the professing church exercises influence or control.

Although the word "Christendom" is not found in the Bible, there are some passages that anticipate the growth of a religious system that although purporting to follow the Lord is far removed from God's purposes. Christendom is a useful label for that state of affairs.

That there should be deterioration and apostasy in the church was predictable. Israel did not remain true to the Lord after their redemption from Egypt and their spiritual condition was at times very poor (1 Cor. 10:5). This accounts for God's judgement in the form of deportation and exile. Likewise during the Lord's ministry large companies of disciples gathered round Him. It is clear however that many were false and did not remain loyal to him (John 6:66).

The Church followed a similar pattern. While initially false professors were exceptional (Acts 8:9-24) by the end of the New Testament there are clear signs that large groups of people were pulling away from the apostles' teaching (2 Tim. 1:15).

We have to rely on history to build up a picture of what happened after the death of the apostles. What we discover is that the Church came to be an organisation of great earthly power. In the period after the conversion of the Roman Emperor Constantine in about 300AD Kings and Emperors came to fear its influence and throughout the Middle Ages the church was the dominant power in Europe. It was presided over by bishops who exercised control over large numbers of churches. Gradually the bishop of Rome came to be pre-eminent. The bishop of Rome is the man now known as the Pope. In about the 9th century the church split into the Orthodox Church (which dominated the Balkans and Russia) and the Roman Catholic Church (which dominated the rest of Europe). The Roman Catholic Church headed by the Pope was then and remains now the largest denomination in terms of wealth and size.

Christendom – its denominations

The following is a brief survey of the major denominations and movements within Christendom and which operate in the UK.

The Roman Catholic Church

The Roman Catholic Church is the largest "Christian" church and has 1.2 billion members (17.5% of world population) and has grown particularly strong in South America. Its key beliefs are that in the Mass the wafer and wine become the literal body and blood of Jesus. Participation in the Mass communicates grace to the participant. They teach that salvation is impossible without baptism by sprinkling and participation in the Mass. They do not believe that anyone can be sure they are going to heaven until they die. They hold Mary in special regard and teach that she was conceived without sin (the immaculate conception), that she was personally sinless, that she is the mother of God, that she remained a virgin and did not have subsequent children after the birth of Jesus and that she was taken bodily back to heaven. They believe that prayer to Mary is effective. They believe that the Pope is the successor to Peter and that their bishops are part of the apostolic succession. They claim infallibility in matters or doctrine and morals. Although they believe in the deity of the Lord Jesus and His personal sinlessness, they do not accept that salvation is through faith in Christ alone.

The Orthodox Church

The Orthodox Church is the second largest denomination with about 300 million members. It was once part of the Catholic church but split from it in the 11th century AD. It resembles the Roman Catholic Church in many ways but also rejects key Roman Catholic doctrines. It does not accept papal infallibility, the immaculate conception of Mary, the bodily assumption of Mary and purgatory. It accepts the Trinity, the deity and sinlessness of Christ. Its liturgy or mode of worship is highly ceremonial. They use icons, music, incense, candles, sculpture, poetry etc. They believe in transubstantiation of the elements of bread and wine into the literal body and blood of Christ. They do not accept the bible as the final and authoritative word of God. They believe that it and their own traditions are authoritative. Each branch of the Orthodox Church is presided over by a Patriarch. They believe in baptismal regeneration i.e. that baptism imparts new birth. They believe that on confirmation the person is given the Holy Spirit. They do not accept that salvation is by grace through faith alone.

The Anglican Church

The Anglican Church – The Anglican Communion worldwide has about 80 million members. In England Henry VIII broke away from the Roman Catholic Church because the Pope refused to give him a divorce from his wife Catherine of Aragon. The Anglican Church was the consequence of this schism. The reigning king or queen of England is its head. Its ecclesiastical head is the Archbishop of Canterbury. The Anglican Church has churches throughout the world. The Scottish counterpart to the Anglican Church is the Episcopalian Church. At one extreme there are Anglicans that are almost indistinguishable from Roman Catholics and at the other there are those that accept that salvation is through faith in Christ alone. They celebrate the Eucharist, which is a rough equivalent to the Roman Catholic Mass and believe that by some miraculous process the wafer and wine become the body and blood of Christ. They baptise infants by sprinkling, which they believe is necessary for regeneration. Unlike their Roman

Catholic counterparts priests of the Church of England may marry. Their Book of Common Prayer is used worldwide in all their churches. Hence their prayers are not spontaneous but read and repeated from year to year according to the set day. They have a divide between clergy and laity so that dispensing communion and officiating at marriages and baptisms are the preserve of their clergy.

Arguably the two most basic truths of Christianity are salvation through faith and baptism by immersion of the believer. None of the great churches described above hold these truths. The idea that Christians should try to disassociate themselves from error is a scriptural one (2 Cor. 6:14-18). Although unity among believers is an ideal to strive for (John 17:11, 21-22) and division is not to be welcomed, the Reformation demonstrates it may at times be necessary.

Presbyterian Churches

Presbyterian Churches - include the Church of Scotland and the Presbyterian churches in the USA, Canada and Ireland. The Presbyterian Church in Ireland is its second largest denomination and is particularly strong in Northern Ireland. These churches were the by-product of the Reformation which followed Luther's challenge to the Roman Catholic Church. In Europe the result was the emergence of the Lutheran Church. Later through the teachings of men like Calvin and John Knox a number of Reformed churches grew up in Switzerland, France and in Scotland. Scotland's national church, the Church of Scotland is Presbyterian and Reformed. The name "Presbyterian" is derived from the Greek word for elder. Although they have salaried ministers, groups of elders together with the minister govern each church. Each church is part of a district presbytery and overall control is provided by an annual General Assembly. The Church of Scotland practices infant baptism and believe that infants join the church when sprinkled.[13] Although they do not believe that sprinkling results in regeneration they believe it brings the child into the church community – whatever that may mean. Full membership comes at confirmation. Confirmation consists of the person confessing his or her faith publicly. Churches of Scotland vary widely in character – some are evangelical while others are not. In Scotland the Kirk has split on a number of occasions and a variety of other Presbyterian denominations have been created including the Free Church, the United Free Church and the Free Presbyterian Church.

[13] www.churchofscotland.org.uk/about_us/our_faith/joining_the_church.

The Pentecostal movement

The Pentecostal movement is not a denomination as such since Pentecostals are found throughout all major denominations including the Roman Catholic Church. It is a 20th century movement. Their defining belief is that the baptism of the Spirit is a personal experience that occurs either at or after conversion and which empowers the believer and draws him into a closer relationship with God. Most Pentecostals believe that this baptism or "second blessing" is accompanied by speaking in tongues and/or other miraculous gifts. They believe that tongues are not necessarily real languages but are ecstatic utterances. Although there are many sincere believers among the Pentecostals their belief that ecstatic babble is the same as the languages of Acts 2 and 1 Cor. 14 is hard to fathom. They believe the panoply of gifts listed in 1st Corinthians exist today including prophecy and miraculous healing. Some Pentecostals have set up their own churches including The Assemblies of God, the Elim Church, the Apostolic church. Extreme Pentecostalism embraces behaviour that is difficult to distinguish from pagan worship. They fall into trances, they convulse on the floor, they engage in incoherent "speech" – all of which is behaviour characteristic of pagan religions. The more moderate Pentecostal churches are orthodox on salvation, the trinity, the death of Christ, baptism by water and the breaking of bread but otherwise embrace the Pentecostal belief outlined above. None of these denominations practise head covering as taught in 1 Corinthians ch 11.

Christendom – its definition

The following section contains the scriptural definition of the systems described above as Christendom.

The Kingdom of Heaven

In Matthew 13 the Lord Jesus described in a series of parables the kingdom of heaven. These parables examine a number of features of this kingdom. Amongst them is the idea that the kingdom of God is populated by the true and false. Thus among the fields of wheat grow tares. Tares resemble wheat but bear no corn. But despite this the two grow together. This state of affairs continues until harvest time. Likewise the kingdom is likened to a lump of dough into which leaven or yeast has been introduced. Leaven is typically an illustration of evil in scripture and this parable seems to describe the infiltration of evil in the kingdom and its gradual spread through the whole. Likewise the kingdom is likened to a catch of fish. Some of the fish are good – presumably fish that are edible and for which there is a market. But the catch also includes bad fish – ones that are inedible or for which there is no market.

The Great House

Paul spoke of "the great house" in 2 Timothy ch 2. It had a variety of utensils. Some were honourable such as gold cups or silver tongs whereas others were dishonourable such as wooden brushes or clay chamber pots. Paul's basic point is that under one roof there may be Christians who are valuable and bring honour to God while others hinder the work of God and dishonour the Lord. Many think that Paul is describing Christendom.

The Prostitute Church

The vision of Revelation 17 and 18 describes a world system that is religious, military and commercial. The power described is not a nation since its power transcends geographical boundaries. It exercises power over many nations. The references to Babylon suggest that religion as well as commerce and military might are in view since Babylon was the centre of an idolatrous system that dominated the East. Geographically however the reference to the seven hills places the nerve centre of this system in Rome. Although Revelation ch 17 anticipates the future, the foundations of this system are in history. As we have seen the false church began to be built shortly after John's death as Rome became the centre for Papal power and the instigator of persecution against those who opposed her. The martyrs of ch 17 refer not only to those who suffered at the hands of Christendom in the dark and Middle Ages but those who it will persecute in the Tribulation. In the O.T. immorality is used as a figure of speech to describe the religious unfaithfulness of Israel to God. This suggests that the prostitution is a reference to corrupt religious practice. These strands of evidence indicate that ch 17 describes a great religious system that will dominate the earth in end times.

KEY SCRIPTURES

²⁴ Another parable put he forth unto them, saying, The kingdom of heaven is likened unto a man which sowed good seed in his field: ²⁵ But while men slept, his enemy came and sowed tares among the wheat, and went his way. ²⁶ But when the blade was sprung up, and brought forth fruit, then appeared the tares also. ²⁷ So the servants of the householder came and said unto him, Sir, didst not thou sow good seed in thy field? from whence then hath it tares? ²⁸ He said unto them, An enemy hath done this. The servants said unto him, Wilt thou then that we go and gather them up? ²⁹ But he said, Nay; lest while ye gather up the tares, ye root up also the wheat with them. ³⁰ Let both grow together until the harvest: and in the time of harvest I will say to the reapers, Gather ye together first the tares, and bind them in bundles to burn them: but gather the wheat into my barn.

³⁶ Then Jesus sent the multitude away, and went into the house: and his disciples came unto him, saying, Declare unto us the parable of the tares of the field. ³⁷ He answered and said unto them, He that soweth the good seed is the Son of man; ³⁸ The field is the world; the good seed are the children of the kingdom; but the tares are the children of the wicked *one*; ³⁹ The enemy that sowed them is the devil; the harvest is the end of the world; and the reapers are the angels. ⁴⁰ As therefore the tares are gathered and burned in the fire; so shall it be in the end of this world. ⁴¹ The Son of man shall send forth his angels, and they shall gather out of his kingdom all things that offend, and them which do iniquity; ⁴² And shall cast them into a furnace of fire: there shall be wailing and gnashing of teeth. ⁴³ Then shall the righteous shine forth as the sun in the kingdom of their Father. Who hath ears to hear, let him hear.

The Kingdom of Heaven – the wheat and tares

³¹ Another parable put he forth unto them, saying, The kingdom of heaven is like to a grain of mustard seed, which a man took, and

KEY SCRIPTURES

sowed in his field: [32] Which indeed is the least of all seeds: but when it is grown, it is the greatest among herbs, and becometh a tree, so that the birds of the air come and lodge in the branches thereof.

The Kingdom of Heaven – the great tree

[33] Another parable spake he unto them; The kingdom of heaven is like unto leaven, which a woman took, and hid in three measures of meal, till the whole was leavened.

The Kingdom of Heaven – leaven in bread

[47] Again, the kingdom of heaven is like unto a net, that was cast into the sea, and gathered of every kind: [48] Which, when it was full, they drew to shore, and sat down, and gathered the good into vessels, but cast the bad away. [49] So shall it be at the end of the world: the angels shall come forth, and sever the wicked from among the just, [50] And shall cast them into the furnace of fire: there shall be wailing and gnashing of teeth.

The Kingdom of Heaven - fish in the sea
Extracts from Matthew ch 13.

[15] Study to shew thyself approved unto God, a workman that needeth not to be ashamed, rightly dividing the word of truth. [16] But shun profane *and* vain babblings: for they will increase unto more ungodliness. [17] And their word will eat as doth a canker: of whom is Hymenaeus and Philetus; [18] Who concerning the truth have erred, saying that the resurrection is past already; and overthrow the faith of some. [19] Nevertheless the foundation of God standeth sure, having this seal, The Lord knoweth them that are his. And, Let every one that nameth the name of Christ depart from iniquity. [20] But in a great house there are not only vessels of gold and of silver, but also of wood and of earth; and some to honour, and some to dishonour. [21] If a man therefore purge himself from these, he shall be a vessel unto honour, sanctified, and meet

 **KEY SCRIPTURES**

for the master's use, *and* prepared unto every good work.

2 Tim. 2:15–21

³ And he carried me away in the Spirit into a wilderness, and I saw a woman sitting on a scarlet beast that was full of blasphemous names, and it had seven heads and ten horns. ⁴ The woman was arrayed in purple and scarlet, and adorned with gold and jewels and pearls, holding in her hand a golden cup full of abominations and the impurities of her sexual immorality. ⁵ And on her forehead was written a name of mystery: "Babylon the great, mother of prostitutes and of earth's abominations." ⁶ And I saw the woman, drunk with the blood of the saints, the blood of the martyrs of Jesus.

⁹ And here *is* the mind which hath wisdom. The seven heads are seven mountains, on which the woman sitteth. ¹⁰ And there are seven kings: five are fallen, and one is, *and* the other is not yet come; and when he cometh, he must continue a short space. ¹¹ And the beast that was, and is not, even he is the eighth, and is of the seven, and goeth into perdition. ¹² And the ten horns which thou sawest are ten kings, which have received no kingdom as yet; but receive power as kings one hour with the beast. ¹³ These have one mind, and shall give their power and strength unto the beast.

¹⁵ And the angel said to me, "The waters that you saw, where the prostitute is seated, are peoples and multitudes and nations and languages.

¹⁸ And the woman that you saw is the great city that has dominion over the kings of the earth."

Rev. 17:1–6, 9-13, 15, 18

KEY QUOTES

Babylon is a system of religion. The Roman Church is likewise. Any relation to the two can only be shown by demonstrating that Babylonian religion is presently practiced by the Roman Church. This has been conclusively done by Alexander Hislop in his book *The Two Babylons*, and need not be reproduced here. Its principal feature (stemming from Nimrod's wife Semiramus and son Tammuz) was that of the cult of mother-child worship. This appeared in one form or another in Babylon, Phoenicia, Pergamos, Egypt, Greece, and Rome. It came into the experience of Israel through Jezebel and is severely condemned by the prophet Jeremiah (44:16–19, 25). The Emperor Constantine, who like the Caesars was the Pontifex Maximus, introduced it into the Christian church when he sanctioned Christianity in A.D. 312. Pagan Romans kept right on worshipping their mother-child god and following the same rituals of Babylon under the name of Christianity. The similarities to that which is perpetuated by the Roman Church are too clear not to see Rome as the pillar church in the final form of apostate Christendom (17:9–10).[14]

Charles Caldwell Ryrie

The history of the church has demonstrated that apostate Christendom is unsparing in its persecution of those who attempt to maintain a true faith in Jesus Christ. What has been true in the past will be brought to its ultimate in this future time when the martyrs will be beyond number from every kindred, tongue, and nation. The blood shed by the apostate church is exceeded only by that of the martyrs who refuse to worship the beast in the great tribulation.[15]

John Walvoord

[14] Apostasy in the Church, Bibliotheca Sacra Vol. 121, Page 44.
[15] The Revelation of Jesus Christ pp. 248–249.

KEY QUESTIONS

1. What is the largest Christian denomination?

2. What was the cause of the Reformation?

3. What are the differences between the Church of England and the Church of Scotland?

4. Which churches subscribe to infant baptism?

TOPIC 6 –
The Church and its gifts

 **Key Points**
- Gifts are given by God to enable Christians to serve Him.
- There are no ungifted Christians though some may not use their gift.
- It is possible to have more than one gift.
- Miraculous sign gifts are no longer given by God.
- Gifts are to be distinguished from natural talents.

Gift - Defined

A gift is something of value that is given freely by a donor to a recipient. The Bible teaches that God gives many gifts (Jas. 1:17). Thus for example He gives the gift of eternal life (Rom. 6:23) and the gift of the Spirit (Acts 2:38). This topic is concerned with a particular class of gifts given by God. These are spiritual gifts given to Christians after salvation which endow them with abilities they would not otherwise have. They include the gift of teaching, the gift of "tongues" (speaking a foreign language without prior tuition), the gift of prophesy and a variety of others.

Gift - Deployed

Those who are saved are meant to serve the Lord Jesus. In order to enable them to serve God effectively He imparts gifts. These gifts are meant to bring blessing to the church of which the recipient forms part, believers generally and the world at large.

Gift - **Described**

The Bible has three main lists of gifts. They are found in Romans 12, 1 Corinthians 12 and Ephesians 4. These lists are illuminating since they reveal that many of the gifts that were in operation in the early church are not ones we are familiar with today. Some gifts are miraculous e.g. the ability to heal, to speak in a foreign language and to interpret. Although some claim to posses these gifts today, the truth is that they have ceased. What passes for miraculous gifts are not the same as the miraculous gifts in use on the Day of Pentecost and for a short time thereafter. That is not to say of course that God's ability to work miracles has been lost. God would be something less than God if He was unable to work miracles. Thus He may in response to prayer perform a miracle. He may exceptionally empower someone for a specific need or occasion. But as a dispassionate scrutiny of the difference between the experience of the early believers and the experience of Christians today will show, God no longer gives believers the gift or ability to do miraculous deeds. He does however continue to provide gifts that are non-miraculous.

Other gifts mentioned in the bible are often treated as human talents or characteristics that may be consecrated to God's service e.g. "helps" and "governments", "he that giveth", "he that showeth mercy". But Paul in 1 Corinthians categorises them as gifts along with other more familiar gifts.

One of the gifts mentioned in 1 Corinthians ch. 12 and Ephesians ch. 4 is the "apostle". This is not a gift in the usual sense at all. An "apostle" is a person not a spiritual ability. Apostles are gifts in a different sense. They were a group of people with unique authority to guide and teach the early Christians. They were given as a gift and once they had been removed they were not given again.

It is often assumed that the gift of prophecy is about foretelling the future. But while many O.T. prophets did foretell the future the greater part of their ministry was connected with revealing God's mind about the present. So too in the N.T. those who prophesied often gave a word direct from God for the present situation. Their gift requires to be contrasted with teaching. Teaching is primarily to do with the task of taking scripture and explaining its meaning. In the early days the scriptures used by the teacher were the O.T. scriptures as the N.T. scriptures had yet to be written. The gift of prophecy overlaps with the gift of teaching since a teacher can seek to apply the word of God and in doing so may bring a word directly from God for that particular situation.

It should be noted that with the end of the apostolic era God ceased to reveal new truth. Over a period of time the writings of the apostles which the early Christians regarded as authoritative were collected along with the writings of some others who were not apostles, such as Mark and James the Lord's half brother and Luke. The letters were made into a collection we call the New Testament scriptures.

Gift - Distributed

What gifts do sisters possess? They may possess all the gifts except those that fit a person to lead in worship or preach publically. The word of God prohibits females from engaging in public prayer, prophesy and teaching (1 Cor. 14:34-35; 1 Tim. 2:12). It is impossible to imagine that God would furnish them with gifts that involved contravention of His own Word. This does not mean that women are unable to speak publically. Most of us have had female school teachers or heard politicians who can express themselves very ably in public. But that ability is a natural one not a spiritual one and if a woman does lead a church in worship or teach publically this is not consistent with the word of God and not an exercise of a gift of the Spirit. 1 Cor. 14:34b points out that this is not peculiar to the New Testament and that the role of women in Israel under Law was not a public one either. There were female prophets e.g. Phillip's four daughters (Acts 21:8); Anna (Lk. 2:36) and Deborah (Judges 4-5). If the Law and the N.T. prohibits women taking a public role then it may be assumed that their prophecies were not in public. It is possible that they did prophesy publically since not everything that is recorded to have been done in scripture necessarily carries God's seal of approval.

Gift - Distinguished

Although some gifts are similar to natural characteristics, they should still be distinguished. While natural talents may be used for God's glory they are not "gifts" in the N.T. sense since they may be possessed by unsaved people. Thus an unsaved person can sing a hymn beautifully but we should not imagine that this is a gift of the sort the Spirit gives believers. Likewise an unsaved musician may play an organ or piano as well as any saved person but the ability is not a spiritual one. Gift should also be distinguished from the fruit of the Spirit which, by contrast with gift, ought to be seen in all Christians.

Gift - Developed

When is gift given? Timothy's gift was apparently given some time after his conversion (1 Tim. 4:14; 2 Tim. 1:6). It is not clear whether Timothy's experience is typical. Some gifts may be given at conversion and develop thereafter. It may be difficult to say with certainty when gifts are given since there may be no immediate evidence of their existence and they may become apparent over time. But young Christians in particular should be keen to know what particular ability or abilities God has given them that will enable them to serve the Lord. Some abilities become obvious very quickly, others take time to develop. Whatever gifts a believer has they should be cultivated. The gift of preaching for example requires a good knowledge of scripture and study is necessary to learn God's word. No one should make the mistake of thinking that gift is only for men and consists in preaching or teaching. All gifts should be valued and appreciated (1 Cor. 12:14-25).

KEY SCRIPTURES

4 For as in one body we have many members, and the members do not all have the same function, 5 so we, though many, are one body in Christ, and individually members one of another. 6 Having gifts that differ according to the grace given to us, let us use them: if prophecy, in proportion to our faith; 7 if service, in our serving; the one who teaches, in his teaching; 8 the one who exhorts, in his exhortation; the one who contributes, in generosity; the one who leads, with zeal; the one who does acts of mercy, with cheerfulness.

Rom. 12:4-8 (E.S.V.)

 **KEY SCRIPTURES**

But every man hath his proper gift of (i.e. from) God, one after this manner, and another after that.

1 Cor. 7:7

4 Now there are varieties of gifts, but the same Spirit; 5 and there are varieties of service, but the same Lord; 6 and there are varieties of activities, but it is the same God who empowers them all in everyone. 7 To each is given the manifestation of the Spirit for the common good. 8 For to one is given through the Spirit the utterance of wisdom, and to another the utterance of knowledge according to the same Spirit, 9 to another faith by the same Spirit, to another gifts of healing by the one Spirit, 10 to another the working of miracles, to another prophecy, to another the ability to distinguish between spirits, to another various kinds of tongues, to another the interpretation of tongues. 11 All these are empowered by one and the same Spirit, who apportions to each one individually as he wills.

1 Cor. 12:4–11 (E.S.V.)

27 Now you are the body of Christ and individually members of it. 28 And God has appointed in the church first apostles, second prophets, third teachers, then miracles, then gifts of healing, helping, administrating, and various kinds of tongues.

1 Cor. 12:27–28

11 And he gave some, apostles; and some, prophets; and some, evangelists; and some, pastors and teachers; 12 For the perfecting of the saints, for the work of the ministry, for the edifying of the body of Christ:

Eph. 4:11–12

22 But the fruit of the Spirit is love, joy, peace, longsuffering, gentleness, goodness, faith, 23 Meekness, temperance:

Gal. 5:22–23

KEY SCRIPTURES

¹⁴ Do not neglect the gift that is in you, which was given to you by prophecy with the laying on of the hands of the eldership.

1 Tim. 4:14

⁶ Wherefore I put thee in remembrance that thou stir up the gift of God, which is in thee by the putting on of my hands.

2 Tim. 1:6

 KEY QUOTES

Christendom has developed the clerical system in which one man has almost the sole responsibility for preaching weekly. That is not based on Bible teaching for, in New Testament times, various men ministered to God's people. Indeed, every believer had some part to play, for the assembly is likened to a human body with each member contributing. Everyone has a spiritual gift that has to be employed for the good of the whole body. To pay one man to have exclusive responsibility for helping God's people is to deny the 'body of Christ' aspect of the local church, 1 Cor. 12. 27.

Jack Hay[16]

Gifts are given with a purpose. First, they promote the unity of the body (1 Cor 12:12-26), for unity within the organism can only be accomplished when every part is functioning properly. Second, they promote the growth of the body (Eph 4:12-16). According to this passage, gifts are given to equip the saints so that they in turn may give themselves to the work of ministering in order that this body will be built up. This building up involves both quantity and quality. Third, they are given to promote the glory of the Head (Col 1:18). This is the ultimate purpose of the organism in its entirety.[17]

Charles Ryrie

[16] Which Church Should I Join and Why? Precious Seed, 2011 Issue 3.
[17] The Pauline Doctrine of the Church Bibliotheca Sacra Vol. 115, Page 62.

KEY QUESTIONS

1. What purpose do gifts serve?

2. What is the difference between a spiritual gift and a natural talent?

3. Which of the gifts mentioned in scripture still exist today?

4. Can gifts develop or wither? If so, why?

TOPIC 7 -
The Church and Its Ordinances

Key Points

- There are three Church ordinances – baptism, breaking of bread and headcovering.

- An ordinance is a symbolic act.

- The ordinances in themselves do not bring spiritual blessing but if observed in faith and with an appreciation of their meaning they are of great value.

What is an "ordinance" of the Church? Usually "ordinance" means a command or order (e.g. Eph. 2:15). In this sense the Church has been given many ordinances e.g. "go ye into all the world and preach the gospel" (Mk. 16:15), "let your woman keep silence" (1 Cor. 14:34) and "let all your things be done with love" (1 Cor. 16:14). In connection with the church however the word ordinance has come to have a narrower meaning and signifies an act the church is commanded to do which symbolises some aspect of the gospel or spiritual truth. Some denominations such as the Roman Catholic Church call the ordinances "sacraments" and believe they communicate salvation or "grace" to the participant e.g. baptism, the Eucharist (the Mass). They also practise ordinances that are not found in scripture such as penance. But scripture teaches that no ordinance or sacrament can alter the spiritual state of the participants. Taking communion does not make an unsaved man any more acceptable to God. Faith alone is the basis of God's blessing. Most evangelical churches teach that baptism and the Lord's Supper are the only church ordinances but I see no reason why headcovering should not also be regarded as an ordinance.

What value do ordinances have? There are a number of possible answers. Publically they symbolise truths that are too important to be left to words. Personally they strengthen faith since they remind the Christian of what is important in life.

Baptism

Matt. 28:19 shows that the Lord Jesus commanded His disciples to preach the gospel and to baptise those that were converted. In the Acts of the Apostles the early evangelists such as Peter, Philip and Paul are all recorded to have obeyed the Lord's command.

Baptism is the English translation of a Greek word that means to immerse or dip. It is to be contrasted with another Greek word rhantízō that means to "sprinkle". The word baptise therefore requires immersion not sprinkling. Further support for baptism by immersion is found in the descriptions of baptism in the Bible. Thus Jesus was baptised in the Jordan River (Mark 1:9). The passage says "He came up out of the water...". Likewise in Acts 8 when the Ethiopian eunuch was baptised we read in verse 38 "they both went down into the water, Philip and the eunuch, and he baptised him. And when they came up out of the water...". It is hard to see why either Jesus or the Ethiopian eunuch should have been in the water if all that was needed was a few drops of water on their heads.

In Rom. 6:4 it is stated "We were buried therefore with him by baptism into death, so that as Christ was raised from the dead by the glory of the Father, we too might walk in newness of life." It is easy to see the parallel between someone disappearing below water and then rising out of the water again. Baptism therefore symbolizes the believer's death and burial to sin and their resurrection to new life in Christ. It also links this change of state to the basis of it – the death and resurrection of Christ. It is also an anticipation of the resurrection of the body at the return of Christ.

Water of itself accomplishes nothing. Being baptised assures no one of heaven. Those that believe baptism is a sacrament make the mistake of thinking that baptism of itself makes a spiritual change to the participant.

The practice in the N.T. is that baptism follows confession of faith. The people "confessing their sins" were baptised by John (Mt. 3:6). An infant is not able to confess anything because it lacks any consciousness of sin or the ability to respond in faith to Christ. If baptism is meant to depict an inward experience accompanying salvation only those who have been converted should be baptised. It is sometimes pointed out that households were baptised in the Acts (Acts 10:44, 46; 16:15, 34) and it is argued that households must include children. But that is untrue. A household may or may not have children, it all depends on the household. In the case of the family of Cornelius the household all spoke with tongues and magnified God. In Acts 16:34 the jailer's household "rejoiced" – these responses would not be expected of little children. We do not even know that Lydia was married. Her household may have been her slaves or the employees in her business.

Breaking of Bread

The day before He was crucified the Lord Jesus celebrated the Passover with his disciples. After they had eaten, He took a loaf of bread and a cup as emblems of His body and blood and asked them to partake of another memorial supper. It would not commemorate Israel's deliverance through the blood of the Passover lamb but the redemption accomplished by His death.

The church has commemorated the Lord's death by breaking the bread and drinking the cup ever since. The bread represents His body. The wine in the cup represents His blood. In eating and drinking the church depicts its dependence on Him. As food nourishes the body so the life and death of Christ nourishes the soul. As food sustains physical life so the life and death of Christ supports spiritual life.

The command "this do in remembrance of Me" makes the Lord's Supper an ordinance. It has no sacramental value. Partaking of itself does not bring the person closer to heaven. If partaken in faith however it strengthens the ties that unite Christians and displays the assembly's appreciation of the Lord Jesus and His death on the cross.

Headcovering

Headcovering is different in a number of ways from the other ordinances. It is required only of women whereas the other ordinances are for everyone. It is not designed to highlight the death of Christ but to underline how God has ordered relations between the male and female in creation and between mankind and God.

While baptism and the breaking of bread were unknown in the O.T. headcovering was practiced – but in a mirror image of its N.T. form. In the O.T. the male priests covered their head while in the tabernacle or temple whereas in the N.T. the males uncover their heads while in the "house of God".

Connected to the covered head of the woman and the uncovered head of the man is the hair covering. Again the symbol varies according to sex. The woman has long hair and the male has short hair (1 Cor. 11:15). Because it is a symbol for everyday life it may not be correct to call the long hair of the woman and the short hair of the man a church ordinance.

 ## KEY SCRIPTURES

Jesus came and spake unto them, saying, All power is given unto me in heaven and in earth. [19] Go ye therefore, and teach all nations, baptising them in the name of the Father, and of the Son, and of the Holy Ghost: [20] Teaching them to observe all things whatsoever I have commanded you: and, lo, I am with you alway, *even* unto the end of the world. Amen.

Mt 28:18–20

As they went on *their* way, they came unto a certain water: and the eunuch said, See, *here is* water; what doth hinder me to be baptised? [37] And Philip said, If thou believest with all thine heart, thou mayest. And he answered and said, I believe that Jesus Christ is the Son of God. [38] And he commanded the chariot to stand still: and they went down both into the water, both Philip and the eunuch; and he baptised him.

Acts 8:36–38

[3] Know ye not, that so many of us as were baptised into Jesus Christ were baptised into his death? [4] Therefore we are buried

KEY SCRIPTURES

with him by baptism into death: that like as Christ was raised up from the dead by the glory of the Father, even so we also should walk in newness of life. [5] For if we have been planted together in the likeness of his death, we shall be also *in the likeness* of *his* resurrection: [6] Knowing this, that our old man is crucified with *him*, that the body of sin might be destroyed, that henceforth we should not serve sin. [7] For he that is dead is freed from sin. [8] Now if we be dead with Christ, we believe that we shall also live with him: [9] Knowing that Christ being raised from the dead dieth no more; death hath no more dominion over him. [10] For in that he died, he died unto sin once: but in that he liveth, he liveth unto God.

Rom 6:3–10

[12] Buried with him in baptism, wherein also ye are risen with *him* through the faith of the operation of God, who hath raised him from the dead.

Col 2:12

[26] And as they were eating, Jesus took bread, and blessed *it*, and brake *it*, and gave *it* to the disciples, and said, Take, eat; this is my body. [27] And he took the cup, and gave thanks, and gave *it* to them, saying, Drink ye all of it[18]; [28] For this is my blood of the new testament, which is shed for many for the remission of sins. [29] But I say unto you, I will not drink henceforth of this fruit of the vine, until that day when I drink it new with you in my Father's kingdom.

Mt 26:26–29

[16] The cup of blessing which we bless, is it not the communion of the blood of Christ? The bread which we break, is it not the communion of the body of Christ? [17] For we *being* many are one bread, *and* one body: for we are all partakers of that one bread.

1 Cor. 10:16–17

---

[18] "Each of you drink from it", N.L.T.; "Drink of it, all of you," E.S.V.

KEY SCRIPTURES

23 For I have received of the Lord that which also I delivered unto you, That the Lord Jesus the *same* night in which he was betrayed took bread: 24 And when he had given thanks, he brake *it*, and said, Take, eat: this is my body, which is broken for you: this do in remembrance of me. 25 After the same manner also *he took* the cup, when he had supped, saying, This cup is the new testament in my blood: this do ye, as oft as ye drink it, in remembrance of me. 26 For as often as ye eat this bread, and drink this cup, ye do shew the Lord's death till he come.

1 Cor. 11:23–26

2 Now I praise you, brethren, that ye remember me in all things, and keep the ordinances, as I delivered *them* to you. 3 But I would have you know, that the head of every man is Christ; and the head of the woman *is* the man; and the head of Christ *is* God. 4 Every man praying or prophesying, having *his* head covered, dishonoureth his head. 5 But every woman that prayeth or prophesieth with *her* head uncovered dishonoureth her head: for that is even all one as if she were shaven. 6 For if the woman be not covered, let her also be shorn: but if it be a shame for a woman to be shorn or shaven, let her be covered. 7 For a man indeed ought not to cover *his* head, forasmuch as he is the image and glory of God: but the woman is the glory of the man. 8 For the man is not of the woman; but the woman of the man. 9 Neither was the man created for the woman; but the woman for the man. 10 For this cause ought the woman to have power on *her* head because of the angels. 11 Nevertheless neither is the man without the woman, neither the woman without the man, in the Lord. 12 For as the woman *is* of the man, even so *is* the man also by the woman; but all things of God. 13 Judge in yourselves: is it comely that a woman pray unto God uncovered? 14 Doth not even nature itself teach you, that, if a man have long hair, it is a shame unto him? 15 But if a woman have long hair, it is a glory to her: for *her* hair is given her for a covering. 16

KEY SCRIPTURES

But if any man seem to be contentious, we have no such custom, neither the churches of God.

1 Cor. 11:2–16

KEY QUOTES

A *symbol* is the sign, or visible representation, of an invisible truth or idea; as for example, the lion is the symbol of strength and courage, the wedding ring of marriage, and the flag of country. Symbols may teach great lessons; as Jesus' cursing the barren figtree taught the doom of unfruitful Judaism, and Jesus' washing of the disciples' feet taught his own coming down from heaven to purify and save, and the humble service required of his followers. A *rite* is a symbol which is employed with regularity and sacred intent.... An *ordinance* is a symbolic rite which sets forth the central truths of the Christian faith, and which is of universal and perpetual obligation. Baptism and the Lord's Supper are rites which have become ordinances by the specific command of Christ and by their inner relation to the essential truths of his kingdom.[19]

Augustus Strong

Baptism as an ordinance is commanded and commissioned by the Lord Himself in the Gospels. It is practised by the evangelists, whose activities are recorded in the book of the Acts. It is expounded doctrinally by the apostles in the epistles of the New Testament. We note, moreover, that believer's baptism was not mentioned until after the resurrection of the Lord, whereas the Lord's Supper was instituted prior to His death. This is significant, for baptism represents not Christ's death for us, but our death with Him.

Gabriel Fyfe[20]

[19] Systematic Theology p. 930.
[20] Precious Seed 1975 vol. 26.

1. What is an ordinance?

2. What value do they have?

3. What truths does baptism teach?

4. What is the symbolism behind the covered head of a woman and the uncovered head of the man in church gatherings?